HI NEIGHBOR
in
OCEANIA

Story by: Uncle Jim

Edited by: Bella Masapolli Wilgus

With Research by:
Wendy Grace Wilgus

Wild Goose
Foxborough Village
15 Mariposa Place
Old Bridge, New Jersey 08857
Visit our website at *www.wendysmarketplace.com*

ISBN: 979-8-9871120-4-5
eISBN: 979-8-9871120-5-2

This book is dedicated to all those who make our local zoos, museums and aquariums possible. Thanks to the Administrators, Zoologists, Curators, Veterinarians, Biologists, Aquarists, Residents and Volunteers who have provided a sanctuary where animals of all species can live in peace and learn to get along with their neighbors, even if they are different.

We are also thankful to the philanthropists and donors who help finance these educational and entertaining institutions and their projects. Without their funding, many of the smaller zoos, museums and aquariums would not even exist.

I want to extend a special thanks to my dear friend Arthur Hasegawa for his technical contribution in formatting portions of this book.

This book is also dedicated to my neighbors. I live in a neighborhood that reminds me how friendly and helpful neighbors can be. This is the America I remember as a young boy in the 40's & 50's. Kids actually play in the street, as well as a local field. Their activities will actually make an interesting story someday as I watch them grow up. Every person, animal, place & thing is an inspiration for another story. That keeps me busy. That's the way I like it.

Hi neighbor!

This is the continent of OCEANIA

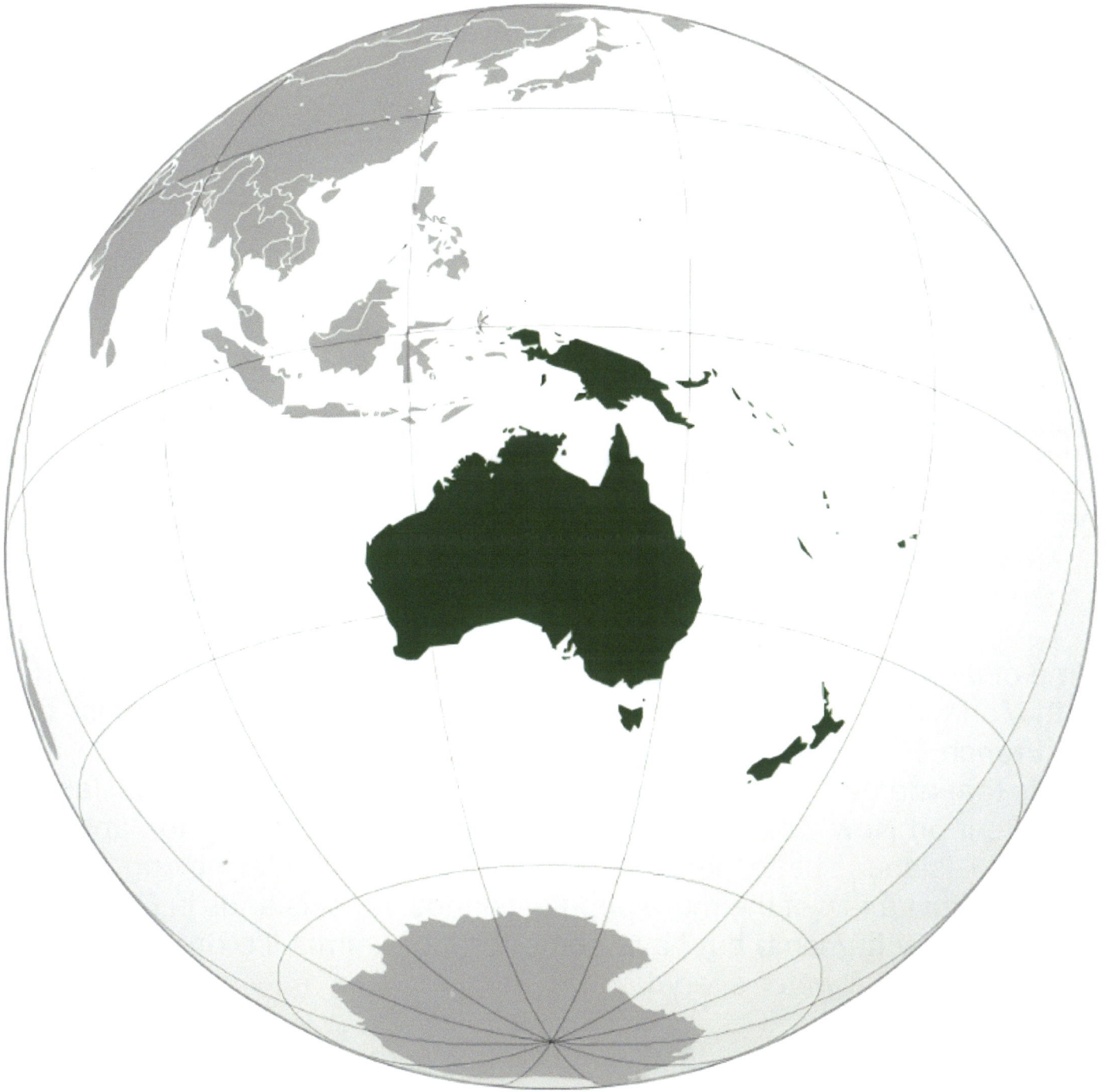

THE CONTINENT OF OCEANIA

The global map on the previous page shows the continent of Oceania on the world globe. Most of the land above water is in the southern hemisphere. The continent extends from New Guinea in the west, the Bonin Islands in the northwest, the Hawaiian Islands in the northeast, Rapa Nui and Sala y Gómez Island in the east and Macquarie Island in the south.

This continent, much of which is underwater, is a geographical region that includes the 4 regions, Australasia, Melanesia, Micronesia and Polynesia. We don't see these names too often because we refer to each country by its political name. The Oceania continent is unique because it consists of thousands of islands throughout the Central South Pacific Ocean. There are 14 independent countries, plus many that are dependent on other countries.

The 14 sovereign nations are Australia, New Zealand, The Federated States of Micronesia, Fiji, Kiribati, Marshall Islands, Palau, Nauru, Papua New Guinea, Tonga, Solomon Islands, Samoa, Tuvalu and Vanuatu.

Some of the dependent countries are Hawaii, American Samoa, Guam in the North Mariana Islands, territories of the United States; New Caledonia, Tahiti and French Polynesia, territories of France; Pitcairn Islands which are 4 islands that are part of the United Kingdom; Cook Island and Niue Island are dependent on New Zealand; the Bonin Islands which belong to Japan, and Rapa Nui Islands, better known as Easter Island, which belong to Chile. These are just a few of the more popular islands. Most islands in Oceania are uninhabited by humans, but have some form of animal life on those islands that remain above water everyday.

Our focus will be on the largest island on this continent, Australia. It not only has an area larger than all the other islands combined, but is one of the most interesting when it comes to unique animals. Australia is just below the equator, and to the extreme west on Oceania. It is south of Asia and north of Antarctica. You are about to meet the most interesting animals in Oceania.

HI NEIGHBOR!

Have you ever dreamed of animals talking to you? That's exactly what happened to me and I can't wait to tell my story. My name is Wendy and my house is on Park Street. It was named Park because the town park was at the end of the street. Inside the park is the most exciting place in the world, our town zoo. My parents have taken me to the zoo many times to see animals from all over the world. But now I will be going on my own. Being on my own will be different, I can feel it. Now that I'm older, they agreed that I'm ready. Today will be my first day. My mom packed a lunch so I could spend the entire day at the zoo. You and I are about to discover the most exciting place in my neighborhood, and who my unique neighbors are.

Henry Vilas Zoo Entrance photo courtesy of Kristin Moala - Modified

I arrived at the zoo just after the gates opened. The first exhibit was home to animals from Australia. Australia is the largest country on the continent of Oceania and has a large variety of animals that are unique to this continent. As I approached the fence a little kangaroo said "Hi neighbor". I said hi, my name is Wendy, what's yours? "My name is Joey. It's nice of you to come visit us today. Are you by yourself?" Oh yes I said, this is my first time at the zoo by myself. "That's very brave of you" said Joey. "Would you like a tour of this exhibit to learn about the animals of Australia?" I was surprised that I was having a conversation with an animal, but didn't hesitate confirming how nice this is.

Joey didn't waste any time and replied, "Let me hop out of here and join you. We can start right here at the kangaroo exhibit. This is my home in the zoo. When visiting the zoo, you should start your journey by reading the sign in front of the exhibit to learn about the animals. Here, see?" as he pointed to a sign. "There are signs in front of every exhibit. These are zoo facts about kangaroos".

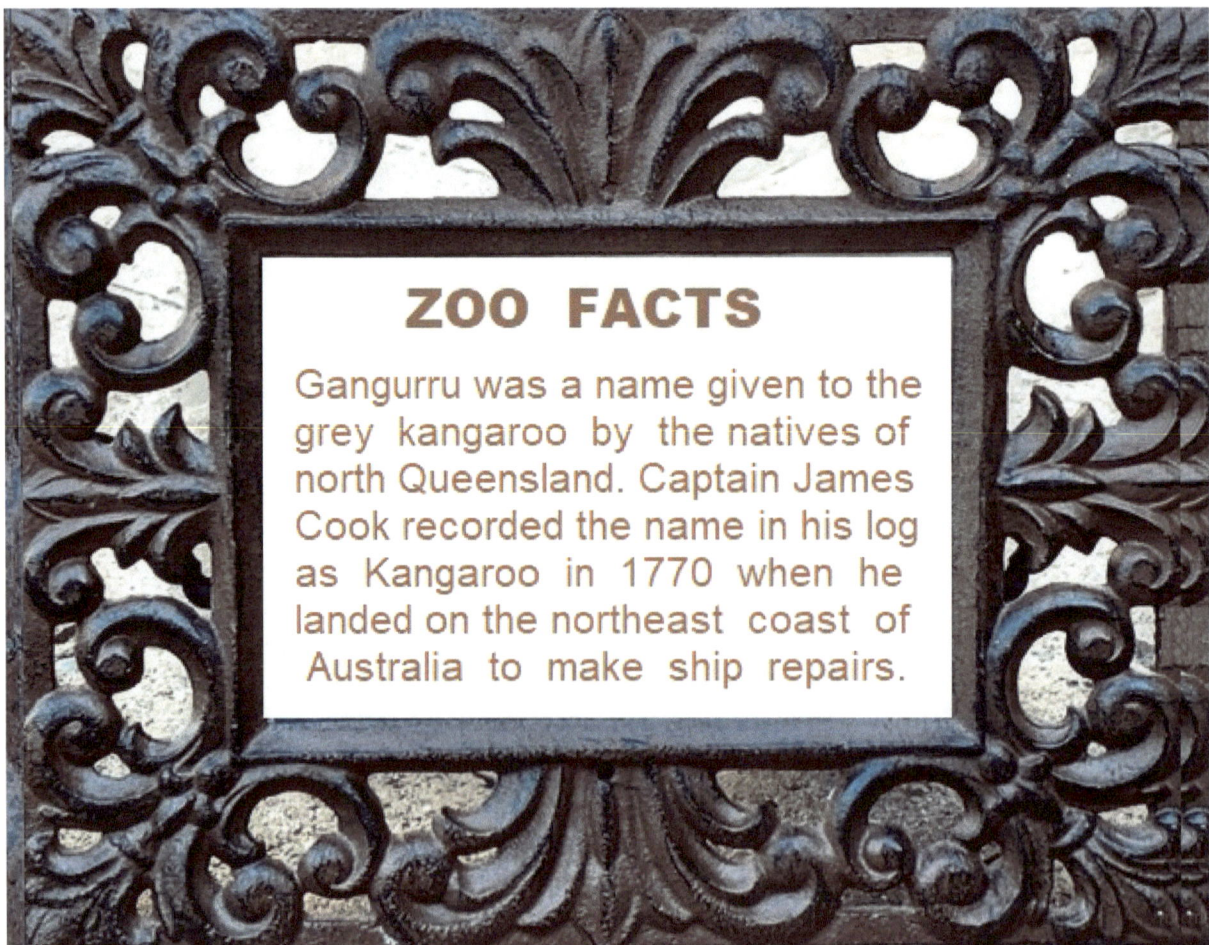

ZOO FACTS

Gangurru was a name given to the grey kangaroo by the natives of north Queensland. Captain James Cook recorded the name in his log as Kangaroo in 1770 when he landed on the northeast coast of Australia to make ship repairs.

See the baby kangaroo in the pouch looking at you? It will live in the mother's pouch until it's old enough to survive on it's own.

Photo courtesy of "Red Kangaroo with Joey" by Mrs. Airwolfhound and is licensed under CC BY-SA 2.0

Oh look, the kangaroo is looking right at us. Joey responded, "That's my mother with my sister in her pouch". Let's say hi neighbor and see what she does. Joey asked "What is a neighbor?" I told him it's someone who lives near you. Like all the living things around you, they're all your neighbors. So Joey and I said together, "Hi neighbor!" Just then she hops toward us and say's "Hi neighbor!" back to us. She suddenly realizes that Joey is outside the fence. "Joey, what are you doing out there?" said his mother. Joey politely said, "I am explaining to my new friend Wendy all about the animals that come from Australia." His mother politely interrupted, "It's nice to meet you Wendy, let me tell you some interesting facts about Kangaroos".

"We are grouped into 3 sizes. The largest is the kangaroo, which is what I am. The medium size is called a wallaroo and the small ones are wallaby. Young one's are called Joey's and remain in the pouch until they are 1 year old. Since Joey is older than one year, he can walk around by himself".

Mother was on a roll as she continued. "Would you believe there are more kangaroos than people in Australia? I am 6 feet tall and weigh 200 pounds. I can jump 9 feet high, 30 feet in distance and run up to 40 miles an hour." I think Joey's mother was exhausted, because she suddenly stopped talking and started hopping away. I didn't even get a chance to say thank you, and to say goodbye.

Joey took over the conversation and said, "My mom must have other things to take care of, so let's say hooroo to my family and visit our neighbors." What does hooroo mean? "Oh, that's how we say goodbye in Australian", said Joey. I also noticed you said 'our neighbors'. I guess when you think about it, we are all neighbors, those who live next door as well as those that live in the area. And don't forget our neighbor towns, neighbor states and even our neighbor countries. When you think about it, we have neighbors all around the world. I wonder, if there were animals on other planets, would they be our neighbors also? Joey chimed in, "I get it Wendy, but let's just go next door for now?"

I laughed as Joey hopped to the next exhibit. I tried to copy him as I hopped behind, but I wasn't as smooth as him. I probably just needed more practice. We reached the next exhibit and there was a koala. Joey yelled "Hi neighbor!" and the little koala came to the end of a branch in the tree where it was eating leaves. The koala spoke back in a sweet voice, "Hi neighbors!" to Joey and me. I told the koala my name was Wendy and it just chuckled. It didn't tell me its name so I guess it didn't have one. Joey suggested that I read the zoo facts so I would know something about the koala.

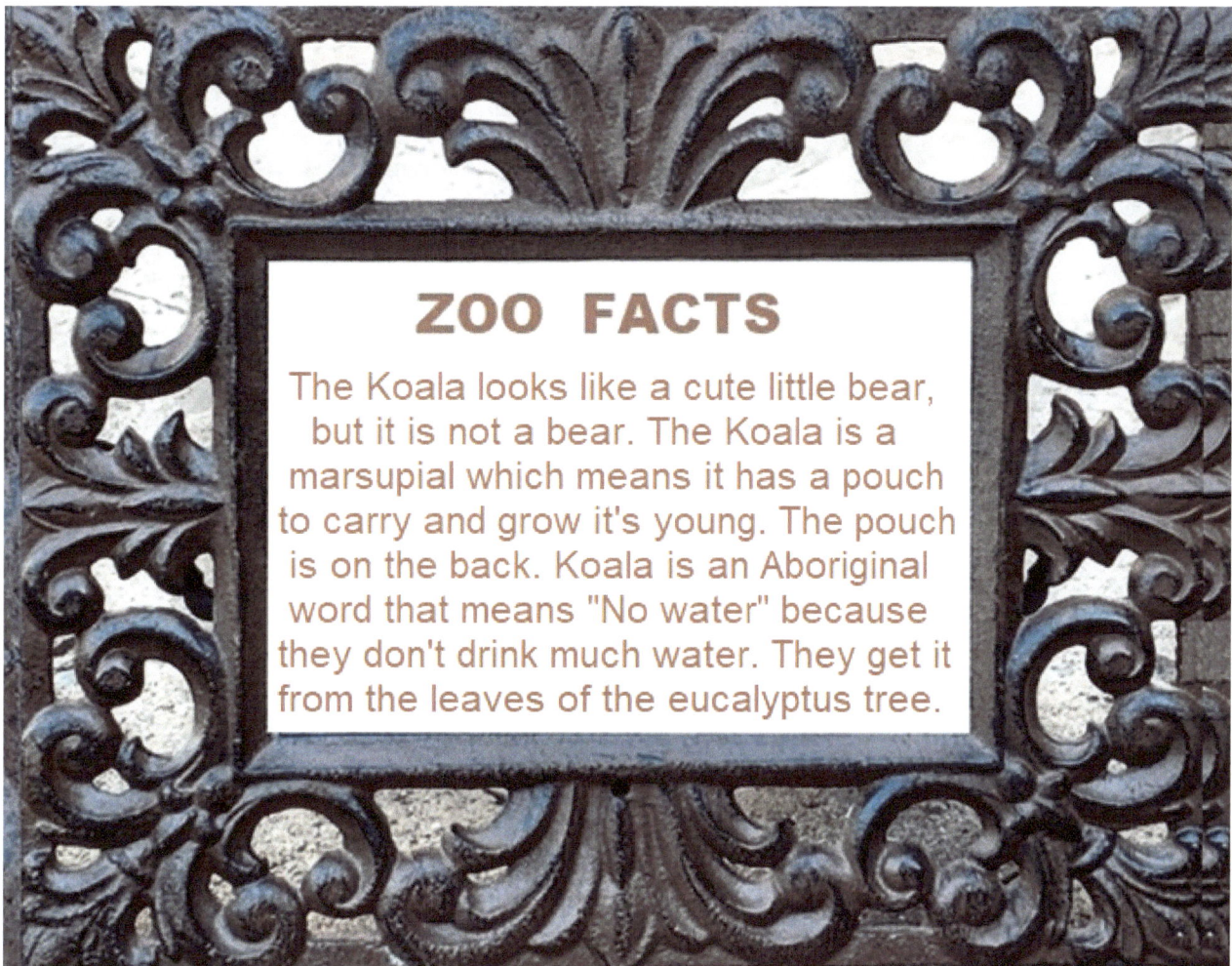

ZOO FACTS

The Koala looks like a cute little bear, but it is not a bear. The Koala is a marsupial which means it has a pouch to carry and grow it's young. The pouch is on the back. Koala is an Aboriginal word that means "No water" because they don't drink much water. They get it from the leaves of the eucalyptus tree.

I asked the koala to tell us something about himself, or herself. I didn't know if it was a boy or a girl.

"Well" said the little koala in a squeaky voice, "I am a girl. I know we all look alike to you but we are all different. My mother could pick me out easily in a mob. I have thick fur, but I am not a bear. I like to sit in the eucalyptus tree eating leaves all day because they taste good and I get all the water I need by eating them. I don't usually climb down to the ground because there are predators, and I don't feel safe there. I sleep almost 20 hours a day right here in the tree. When I was young I slept in my mother's pouch, which happens to be on her back, unlike other marsupials. My mother is 36 inches tall and 25 pounds. I expect to grow as big as her someday and live between 12 to18 years. Do you know there are about 300,000 koala in Australia?

Let me leave you with one more interesting fact, I have a thumb just like you Wendy, as well as long claws, and that helps me climb trees and hold on to a branch while I am sleeping. Look at your hands Wendy and Joey. Which of you has a thumb? I need to go to sleep now."

Koala hang on with sharp claws, even the baby.

Photo courtesy of "koala" by Birdies100 which is licensed under CC BY-NC-SA 2.0

"Bye neighbor", said Joey, "now we are going to hop over to another section and meet a bird that cannot fly, the emu." I looked across the open field and told Joey there was a bird over there with no head. "It may look like that Wendy, but emu dig holes in the ground with their beaks to create nests for their eggs" Joey explained. "Sometimes they'll just be moving eggs around and it looks like a long neck with no head." We yelled "Hi neighbor!" and the emu picked up its head, came running toward us and said, "Hi neighbor!" back to us. It stared at us with gigantic eyes.

Joey and I were surprised when suddenly the emu ran off on two long legs as if we scared it. Joey said they're a little shy. Since it ran off and didn't stick around to tell us about emus, Joey reminded me to read the sign for a little background, then he would elaborate on what he knew about emu's.

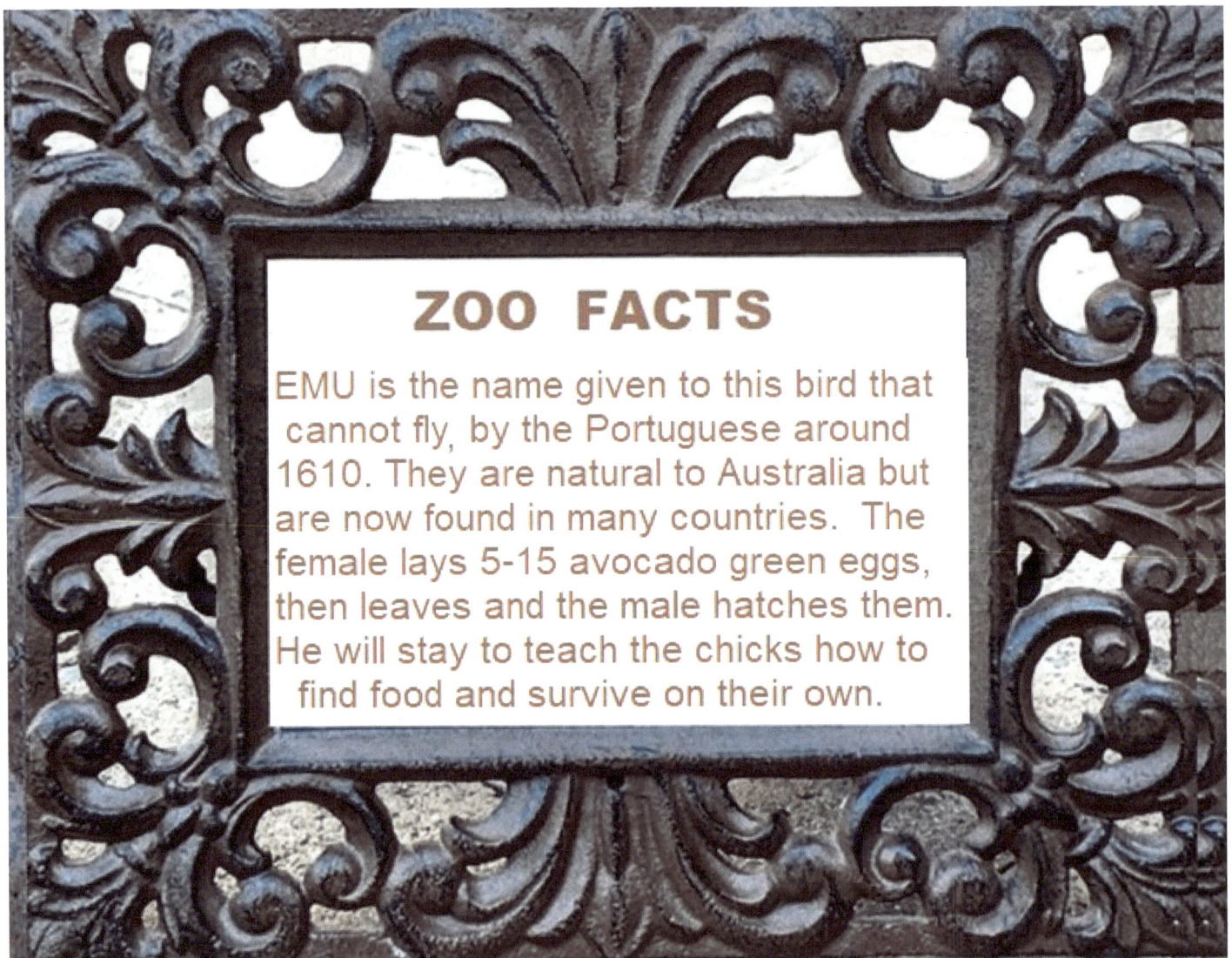

ZOO FACTS

EMU is the name given to this bird that cannot fly, by the Portuguese around 1610. They are natural to Australia but are now found in many countries. The female lays 5-15 avocado green eggs, then leaves and the male hatches them. He will stay to teach the chicks how to find food and survive on their own.

EMU actually eat
small rocks.

"Emu Searching for a Shiny Bit of Stone" by AntoGros is licensed under CC BY 2.0. To view a copy of this license, visit https://creativecommons.org/licenses/by/2.0/?ref=openverse.

"The emu is the second largest bird in the world, after the ostrich. It is 6 feet tall, weighs 100 pounds, can run 30 miles an hour, and can live to 20 years old. There are about 725,000 in the wild right now, plus thousands raised by people on emu farms for food all over the world. They have 3 toes and 2 sets of eyelids, one for blinking and one to keep dust out. Emu have soft fluffy feathers on the body but none on the legs. These birds cannot fly but use their wings to steer when running, as well as flap them to cool off. Baby Emu's are called chicks and are born in an egg, just like a chicken, and actually break the egg themselves from the inside to hatch. Young Emu start growing feathers (plumage) at about three month old. Their diet consists mostly of insects and grass. Oddly, they also eat small stones, like sand, to help break up the food so they can digest it."

Joey, you know so much about emu's. I am impressed. "Oh, thank you Wendy" said Joey. "I visit them almost every day and they tell me all about themselves. But let me tell you a few more facts. Emu have good eyesight and hearing. They have sharp claws on their toes to defend themselves against predators and to dig holes to lay their eggs. They don't sleep more than 90 minutes at a time. They're always on the alert for predators, especially in the wild. They don't drink often, but when they do, they can drink for 10 minutes. In that time they can consume a lot of water"

"That's all I have to say about that" said Joey, "so let's meet the next neighbor."

I'm looking at the Zoo Facts and it looks like there are extra letters in the name. It looks like kookaburra. "You pronounced it perfectly" said Joey.

"In this enclosure is a bird that can fly, the kookaburra. People call its habitat an aviary. It's an enclosure because it prevents birds from flying away, but large enough to allow them to fly as if it were an open space. Since we are not actually in Australia, their home country, they would get lost outside their simulated natural habitat. So the aviary protects them in many ways."

Oh look, here comes a kookaburra now. "Hi neighbor!" Joey and I said. The kookaburra said "Hi neighbor!" and it started laughing, even though no one told a joke. The laughter was so funny, I started laughing also. Suddenly more kookaburras came over and started laughing. It got so loud it was scary. Joey said "we may have to leave or they may never stop laughing." I suggested we stay a little longer because they are so pretty. Suddenly all the birds left but one, and he told us some interesting facts.

ZOO FACTS

Kookaburra are part of the Dacelo species which was introduced by English zoologist William Elford Leach in 1815. Dacelo is the latin word for kingfisher, though Kookaburra seldom eat fish. They primarily eat insects.

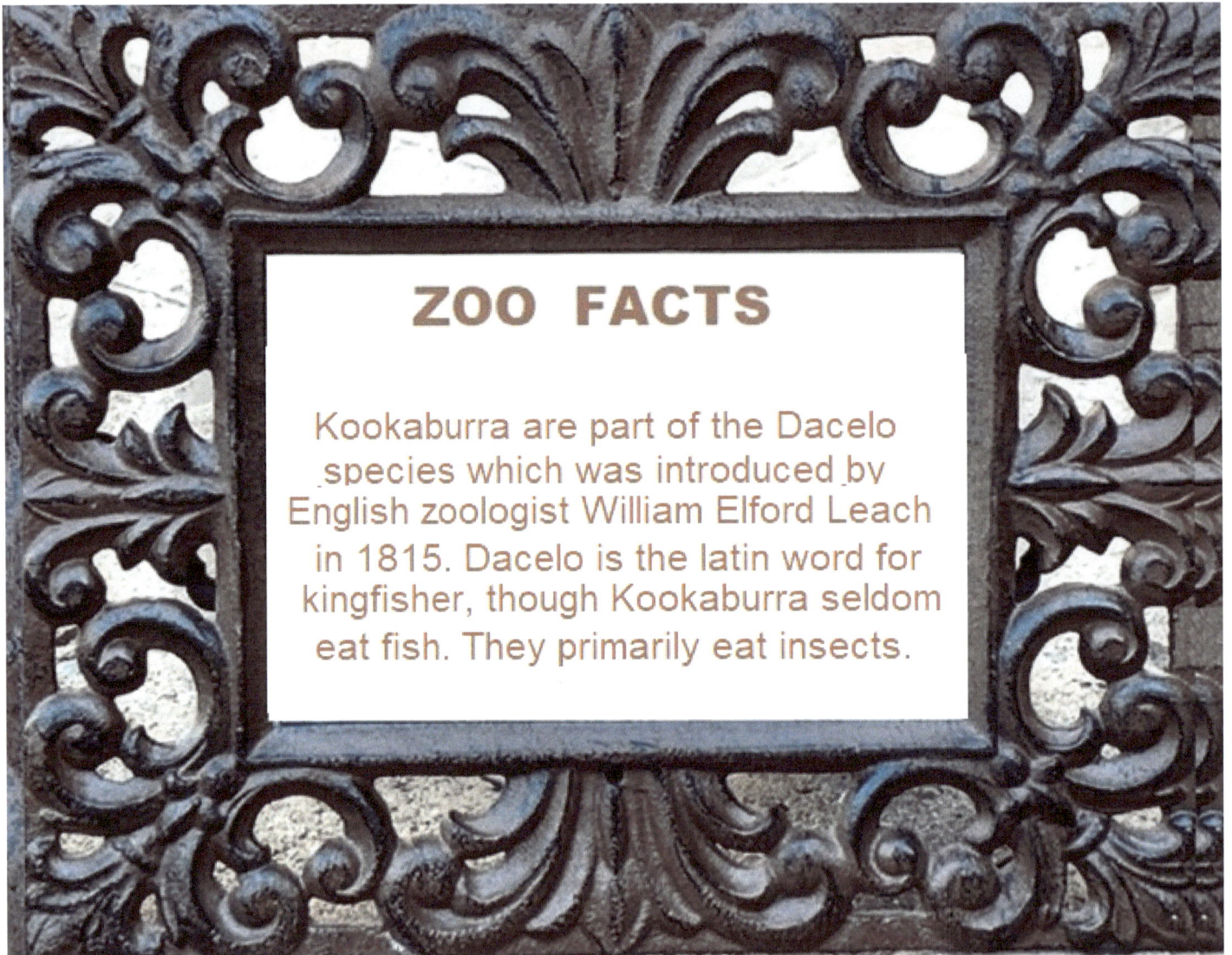

This beautiful bird started talking to us. "We are part of the Kingfisher family of birds. There are 4 types of Kingfisher and the Kookaburra is the largest. I am 19 inches long, weigh a whole pound, and expect to live 20 years. I have light blue wings that can stretch up to 20 inches and an extra-long 4 inch beak. We are basically meat eaters and prefer to eat insects, but will expand our diet and eat rodents and small animals. We live in trees and can swoop down to surprise our prey at 20 miles an hour. I think we're pretty fast."

Kookaburra birds are famous for their laughing sound when they call out. Can you tell me more about this unique habit? "We often get together in groups early in the morning or late in the evening and all start calling at the same time. These calls are known as the "Bushman's Clock". Bushmen are the natives who live in the wild of Australia and this laughter tells them when to wake up and when to go to bed. We are glad that you're interested in our laughing sound." Let's take another look at how colorful this kookaburra bird is and then we can move on.

Do I look like i'm laughing?

"Look Wendy, here is the devil himself." We exchanged greetings as we all said "Hi neighbor!" to each other. I asked the Tasmanian devil if he really is the devil. "No my dear", said the curious looking animal. "When I eat I make a screeching sound and people say it sounds devilish, so they gave me that nickname. It's just a name and all I can do is keep correcting people. I know who I am and I'm not a devil."

Well, you look harmless to me. I read the ZOO FACTS about your species and they sound very interesting. What else can you tell us about yourself?

ZOO FACTS

The name of the Tasmanian Devil came from the first European settlers to visit Australia. They began hearing strange screams and growls from deep within the bush. Settlers believed the sounds were from evil spirits of the devil. Since this was on the island of Tasmania, it became known as the Tasmanian Devil.

They make so much noise when they eat they sound like the devil is screaming.

Photo courtesy of "Tasmanian Devil" by Mathias Appel is licensed under CC BY-SA 2.0

The Tasmanian devil proceeded to tell us about himself. "I'm named after the island where I live, Tasmania. It's about 150 miles off the southern coast of Australia which is on the continent of Oceania. "

"The name Tasmanian Devil is a lot to say so Aussies gave me a shortened nickname, the Tassie Devil. The nickname has been reduced to Tassie, which I like. No more Devil. People will call me by any of these names, but I know I am just an animal surviving in the jungle, with or without a name."

"Babies are called joey, just like the kangaroo or koala baby. A mother can lay 20 to 40 eggs in one litter, but on average about 4 joeys will survive and they will all live in her pouch. Despite our size, we have a strong bite in relation to our body size and we can be ferocious fighters when attacked. We are meat eaters and even eat the bones of animals with our strong teeth. There are about 25,000 living in Tasmania today, but we are an endangered animal due to a rare facial disease and cancer."

"I am 26 inches long plus my 10 inch tail, and weigh about 26 lbs. I can easily out run Wendy, but I'm not sure about Joey. I can run up to 16 miles an hour. I am nocturnal, which means I sleep all day and hunt at night. I often play with my brothers, sisters and my devil neighbors at night when I'm wide awake. There are probably more things about Tassie's that may interest you, but you can look up more facts about us on the internet."

Well, thank you for all that information Tassie. Then Joey and I decided to move on. I turned around and said bye neighbor, you cute little devil. Do you know when I looked at him I saw a smile on his face. Absolutely too cute to be a devil.

"This next animal may look more familiar, maybe even like a house pet. It's called a Dingo and they are wild dogs that run all over the wilderness of Australia, but not on the island of Tasmania," said Joey

"Hundreds of years ago they actually were like any dog and were loyal house pets". Joey continued, "Some Aussies now raise them in preserves trying to keep the breed pure. Dingo can breed with other dogs, but their puppies will not be pure dingoes. They can be trained to be pets, but it is not recommended. Dingo is like a slang name for this gracious looking dog. Look at the zoo facts and you'll be surprised to learn their official name"

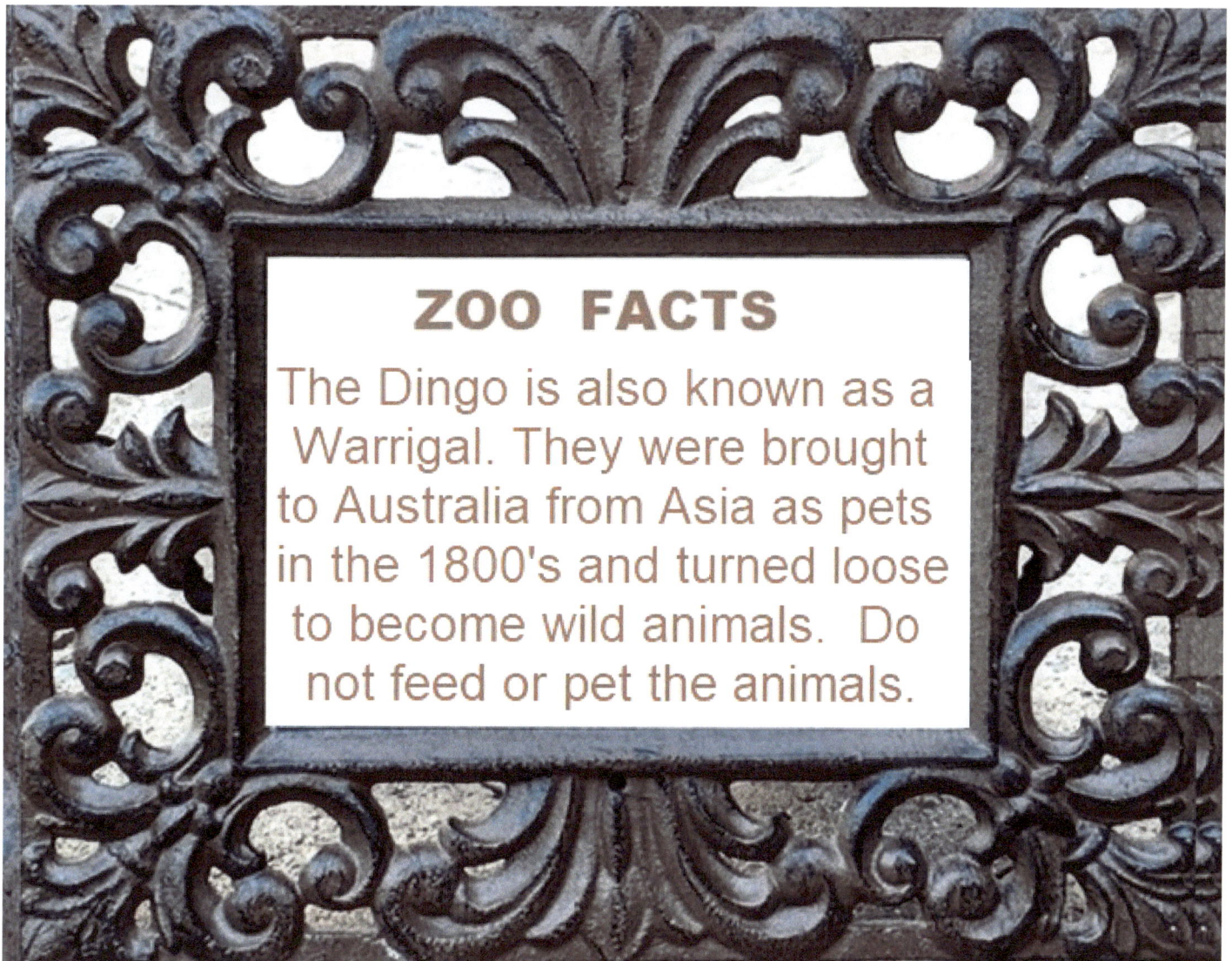

ZOO FACTS

The Dingo is also known as a Warrigal. They were brought to Australia from Asia as pets in the 1800's and turned loose to become wild animals. Do not feed or pet the animals.

Well you're right about two things, they look like house pets and they have an interesting name. Here comes a pack of them. They're so harmless looking. Can I take one home? Joey quickly replied, "Not so fast young lady, they're still considered wild animals."

Wow, look how proud they walk, right toward us, like they want to come home with me. Then the dingo said "Hi neighbor!" before we could say anything. "Well, Hi neighbor to you", we said. Aren't you a friendly little fellow? "Yes" said the dingo, "but please don't believe any nasty rumors about me being ferocious. I have to hunt to eat, and sometimes I have to kill my food to be able to eat it."

"In all modesty, I am a handsome dog, with a bushy tail, sharp ears, long legs and a trim body. Like all dogs, we are members of the grey wolf species, but friendlier looking. Did you know we cannot bark, but howl like a wolf to communicate with other dingoes?"

"We can turn our head 180 degrees and rotate our wrists, which would allow us to turn a door knob with our paws. I'm sure Wendy can do that but Joey can't. Try to rotate your wrist and you'll see what I mean. No other dog can do that. Of course there are no door knobs in the wild, but it comes in handy when eating."

"A male dingo is bigger than the female. I am a male and stand about 2 feet tall, 4 feet long and weigh about 40 pounds. Females give birth to 5-10 pups a year. We usually group in packs of 12 adults to protect the pups, as well as to hunt. My relatives in the wild live about 6 years, but here I am close to 15 years old living in a zoo. I like it here. I have large, sharp teeth which I need to chew meat."

"Of course we are fed very well here at the zoo. In the wild our ancestors hunted for meat. They're excellent scavengers. When necessary they found it easy to hunt sheep. The farmers didn't like that, so they built the longest fence in the world across Australia in the 1920's. It was 3,488 miles. They did a lot of fence repairing so they reduced it to 1600 miles back in 1980."

I remember my geography when I went on a family vacation. 1600 miles is further than driving from Maine to Florida, or California to Texas. That's a long distance. The pack was getting restless so we better go. "Bye neighbors!"

Where is the rest of my pack. I don't like being alone.

"Canis lupus dingo" photo courtesy of Sam Fraser-Smith, marked with CC by 2.0.

This was all so very interesting. Are there anymore neighbors from Australia we can visit? "Yes", said Joey, "there is one more I want you to meet."

"Look at the sign. What does it say?" Wendy had to look at the name carefully to make sure she could pronounce it.

Platypus? What is that?

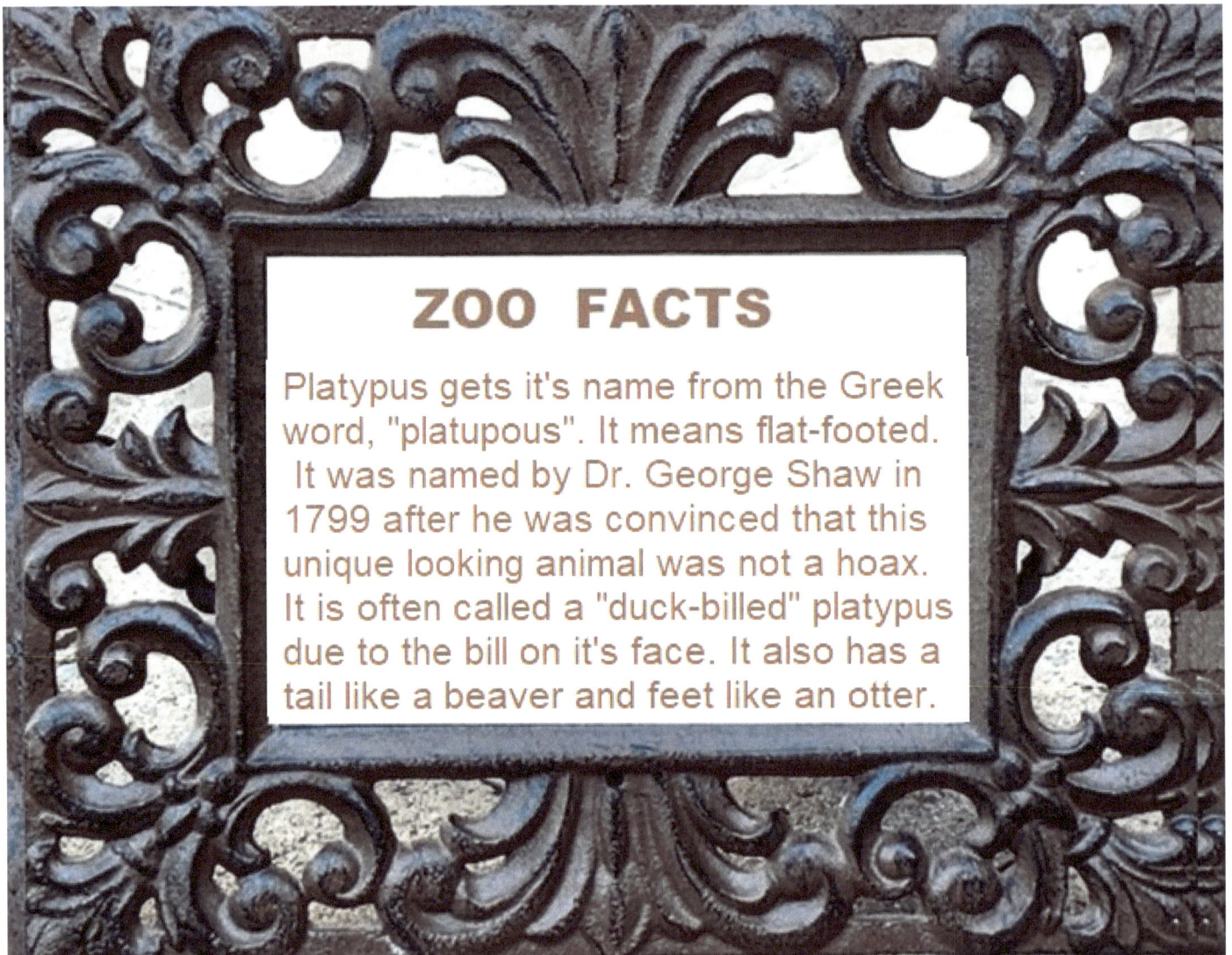

ZOO FACTS

Platypus gets it's name from the Greek word, "platupous". It means flat-footed. It was named by Dr. George Shaw in 1799 after he was convinced that this unique looking animal was not a hoax. It is often called a "duck-billed" platypus due to the bill on it's face. It also has a tail like a beaver and feet like an otter.

"Well, if you look in that pond you'll see an animal scraping the bottom in search of food", said Joey. Platypus is such a funny name, I was trying to imagine what it would look like. When I did see it, I could only describe it like a duck in the front and a beaver in the back. It certainly looks different, unlike any animal I've ever seen. Are you sure you didn't glue two different animals together? "No, of course not", replied Joey. "God made all animals different, like humans are different. That doesn't mean there's something wrong with them".

Photo courtesy of "Feeding Platypus" by Brisbane City Council is licensed under CC BY 2.0

It must have heard us because its head poked out of the water and it walked toward us. We said "Hi neighbor" and, as the tail flapped as if to send a message, it said "Hi neighbor!" back to us. It's a strange looking animal I thought to myself. Look, it has webbed feet like an otter. So this is a platypus?

It didn't stay long and scurried back into the pond where it felt more at home. It was too shy to talk with us. "Don't worry Wendy, I know something about these animals. I visit them almost every day" said Joey.

"I can tell you that platypus are mammals, but unlike most mammals, they lay eggs. The mother digs a tunnel in the mud and she will lay her eggs to have babies. The babies are called puggles, though some people call them platy pups. They have a face like a duck so are often called a duckbill platypus. They're unique with a tail like a beaver and a thick furry body like an otter with webbed feet."

Joey continued. "They have no teeth and no stomach, so they grind their food with horns inside their duckbill. They rely on electric sensors in the duckbill to find food and navigate. The male is about 20 inches long and the female about 16 inches. They are nocturnal which means they sleep in the day and hunt at night. Platypus mostly live in the water and can stay under water up to 2 minutes at a time. Within 2 minutes they must come up to breath air."

"I'm sure there is much more to know about platypus, but that's all I can remember right now" said Joey. That was very informative, thank you for that.

"I hope you learned something about the animals we met today" said Joey. I learned so much today I can't wait to get home to tell my mother and father everything. You've done a wonderful job.

Joey made an interesting observation which he shared with me. He noticed that, although they all look quite different, all these animals had one thing in common. They were all from Australia in a place called Down Under. I thought that was quite interesting. "But there's much more to Oceania than Australia", said Joey.

I told Joey that I was getting hungry and would like to eat. I offered to share my lunch with Joey. He said he only ate plants. I looked at my sandwich and saw there was lettuce with the turkey. I asked Joey if he could eat that and he smiled which meant yes to me. So I gave him my lettuce and we sat in the shade of a tree having lunch together. "While we're resting, let me tell you about other unique animals you might want to read about", said Joey. "In New Zealand there is the Kakapo, a parrot that is too heavy to fly, and the Kiwi, a bird that burrows in the ground. There is also the Tuatara, a reptile whose ancestors go back to the Jurassic Period. They can live well over 100 years. You may also want to look up the Giant Gecko in New Caledonia, as well as the Kagu bird. Then there is the Palila, the largest Hawaiian honeycreeper, a pretty bird that looks like a large finch. On the islands of Fiji you'll find the Crested Iguana. It's unlike any other iguana, with short spiny crests along the back."

After eating, I realized I had a busy morning and was tired. I told Joey I would like to go home to rest, but I could come back next Saturday if my parents would allow. Joey thought that would be great and offered to escort me to the exit. "When you come again, look for me and say, 'Hi neighbor!', then I'll find you. I'll show you more of the zoo each time you come. There is so much to see."

As I left the zoo, we said "Bye neighbor" to each other. Then Joey said, "You are such a nice person. I look forward to seeing you next week." Wasn't that nice of him?

FACTS ABOUT OCEANIA

Water, water, everywhere.
It's a continent full of adventure.
Oceania consists of over 10,000 islands.
There are more sheep in Oceania than people.
The estimated human population in 2022 was 43,365,000.
The population of Australia alone was over 26 million people in 2022.
Mauna Loa in Hawaii is home to the largest volcano on Earth, 2.6 miles high.
Every island country is surrounded by ocean water, which defines their borders.
Some islands are home to Birds Of Paradise which have an elaborate mating dance.
The Blue Whale, Shark, Dolphin, and Orca all reside throughout the waters of Oceania.
The Great Barrier Reef in Oceania is the largest coral reef in the world, about 1600 miles.
Many animals in Australia are unique to that country though some migrate to other islands.
Fletcher Christian landed on Pitcairn in 1790 then set adrift Captain Bligh of HMS BOUNTY.
Located in the middle of Australia is Ayers Rock, the largest rock on the planet, called Uluru.
Oceania is home to unique animals such as the kiwi, kagu, tuatara, kakapo, palila and more.
Saltwater crocodile are found throughout the South Pacific, but none as large as Dominator.
Dominator is the 2nd largest croc ever seen at 20 feet, 2200 pounds and lives in Australia.
The islands are surrounded by salt water and contain a small percentage of fresh water.
Australia is by far the largest island in Oceania and often referred to as a continent.
All baby marsupials born here are called Joey's, whether they are girls or boys.
Quokkas are the size of a cat with teddy bear ears & live on Rottnest Island.
In some of these countries vehicles drive on the left side of the road.
Australia exports more coal than any country in the world.
Oceania has more land than all 50 states in the USA.
Some islands have year round tropical seasons.
Some will have four distinct seasons.
Some are a vacation paradise.
Shrimp on the Bar-B?
Beautiful beaches!

I hope you enjoyed reading this book and learned something about geography and the interesting animals that inhabit the continent of Oceania. Now get ready to enjoy the educational excitement of the other six continents in the **HI NEIGHBOR** series, AFRICA, ANTARCTICA, ASIA, EUROPE, NORTH AMERICA and SOUTH AMERICA. Look for these other adventurous stories where you purchased this book.

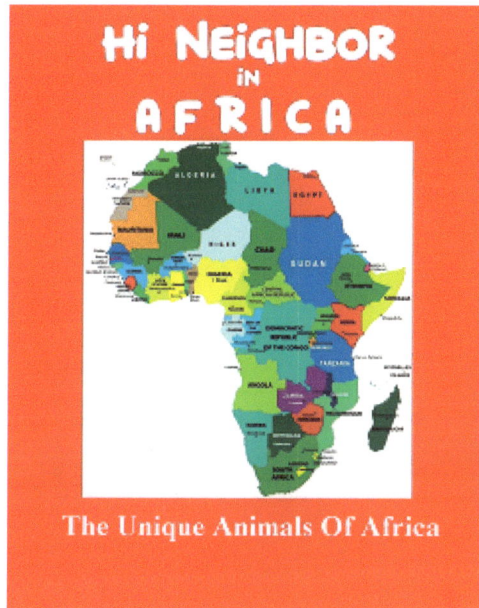

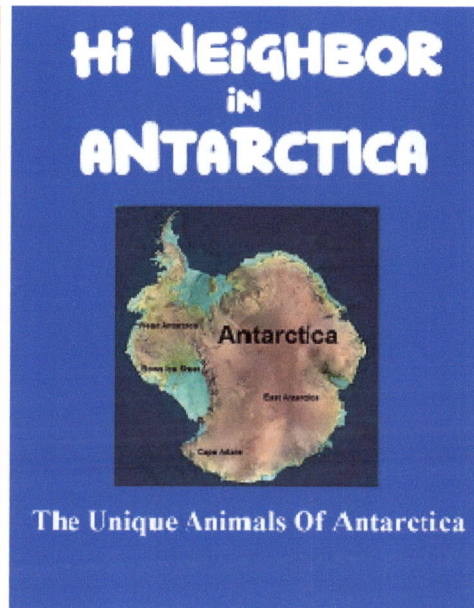

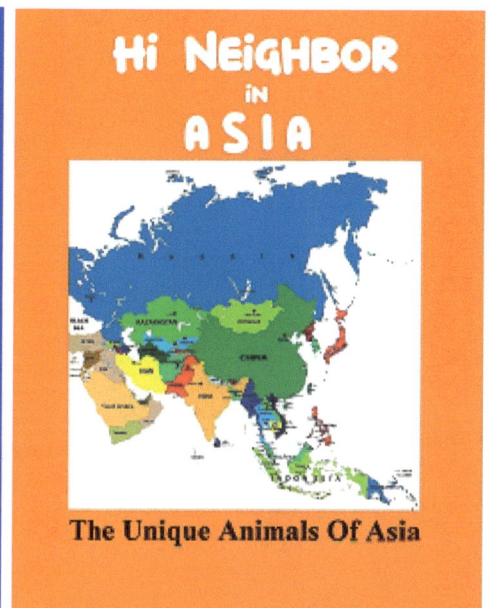

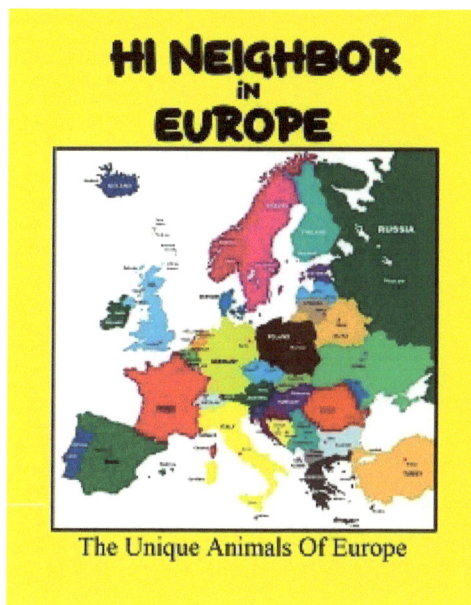

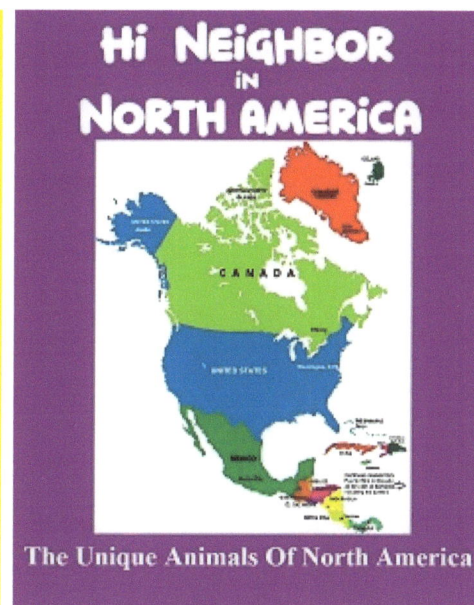

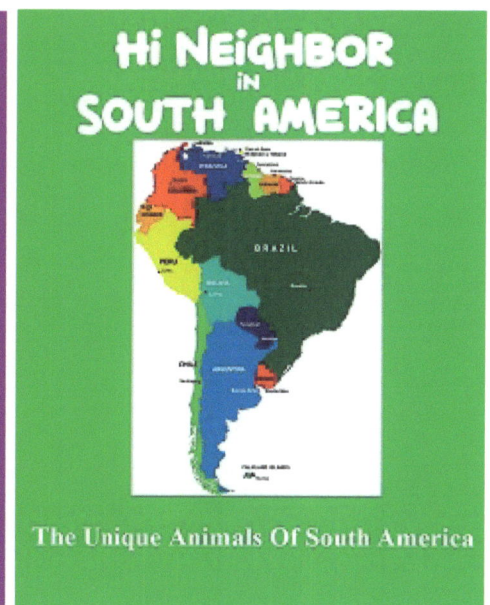

HI NEIGHBOR in AFRICA
The Unique Animals Of Africa

HI NEIGHBOR in ANTARCTICA
Antarctica
The Unique Animals Of Antarctica

HI NEIGHBOR in ASIA
The Unique Animals Of Asia

HI NEIGHBOR in EUROPE
The Unique Animals Of Europe

HI NEIGHBOR in NORTH AMERICA
The Unique Animals Of North America

HI NEIGHBOR in SOUTH AMERICA
The Unique Animals Of South America

Now turn the page to see where all 7 continents are located relative to each other. Remember, the Earth is round and these continents are on the surface of a globe.

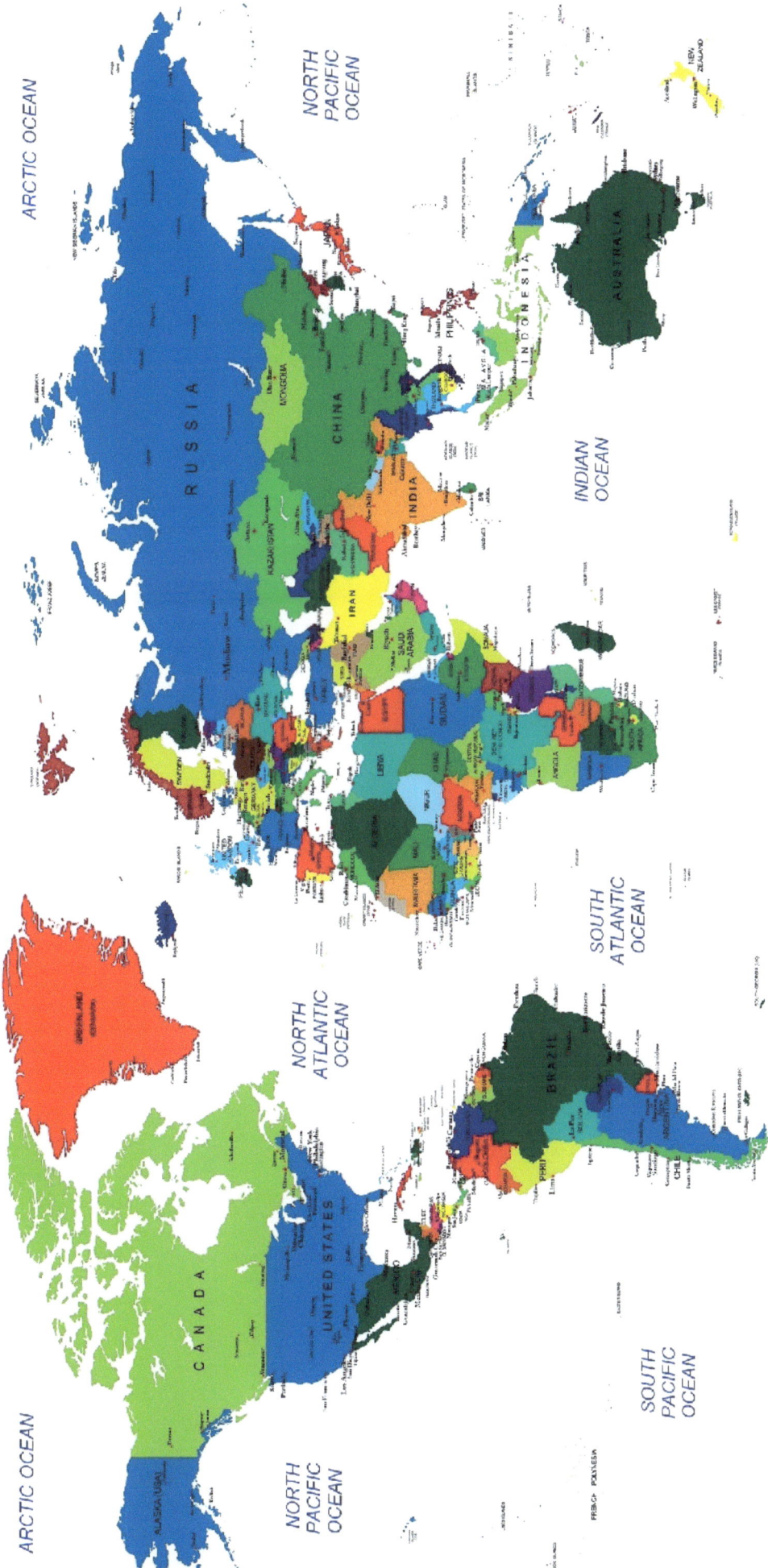

Map of the world showing where each of the seven continents are located.

Appendix

The previous maps are courtesy of the following sources and have been modified to adapt their use in this book: